written in the stars

Poems and Pictures
Diane DiCola

Copyright © 2021 by Diane DiCola.

All rights reserved. No part of this publication may be reproduced, distributed or transmitted in any form or by any means, including photocopying, recording, or other electronic or mechanical methods, without the prior written permission of the publisher, except in the case of brief quotations embodied in critical reviews and certain other noncommercial uses permitted by copyright law. For permission requests, write to the author at Diane@DianeDiCola.com.

Ordering Information:
Quantity sales. Special discounts are available on quantity purchases by corporations, associations, and others. For details, contact Diane@DianeDiCola.com.

Written in the Stars/ Diane DiCola. —1st ed.
ISBN 979-8-9850658-0-0

*In memory of my mother, Stella,
the very first star I laid my eyes upon.*

INTRODUCTION

"We're shakin' up the status quotes, baby!" blurted Uranus, planetary God of Change and Surprise, as he transited my 3rd House which governs writing and communication.

Many years ago, I dreamed I was lying on my back on a magic carpet ride across a velvety black sky. Each constellation twinkled, passing over me quietly as if I were on an amusement park ride with no screaming teenagers or corny music to distract me. I was alone, relaxed and peaceful, enjoying the view of the heavens above. I can't recall anything else about the dream, no special message or meaning to derive, just a lovely moment in time that has stayed with me all these years.

Growing up in the 1970s, my mother and I read our daily horoscopes in the newspaper, consulted dream interpretation books for meanings about our nightly dreams and once went to a fortune teller who read tea leaves. The mystery of the future begged to be revealed although our thirst for that knowledge was never quite satisfied. As an aspiring writer, I wrote stories about kings and queens, song lyrics heavy with teenage unrequited love and poems as assigned by junior high English teachers. My mother and I played Scrabble®, did crosswords and word search puzzles. I didn't know it at the time, but my love of words and a perpetual search for the meaning of life would one day converge like two meteors hurtling through space towards each other destined to collide as a starburst of my own self-expression.

Fast forward to 2020. My mother died in February. A week later, while in Florida on a business trip with my husband, there was an attempted burglary at our home. Shortly after that, we found ourselves with the rest of the world on lockdown. In what appeared to be a scene from a sci-fi novel, a deadly virus simply began stealing away our everyday lives.

In spite of the uncertainty of the virus and of our ways of living being altered by constantly changing government rules, I welcomed the solitude. The pandemic gave me the time to grieve the loss of my mother. As an only child, I had a lot of work ahead of me to sell her house and settle her estate. Fortunately, the love of my husband, family and friends helped me through it all. Another coping mechanism was writing Morning Pages...thanks, Julia Cameron.

In late Summer of 2020, I learned about an online astrology class taught by Heidi Rose Robbins. I'd been a follower of her Moon Notes posted daily on Instagram. Heidi's love of astrology infused with poetry was just the right balm for my weary soul. Beginning each weekly class with a poem or two to set the tone or evoke a mood, Heidi taught us everything we needed to know about esoteric astrology. First, we learned the importance of the Sun, Moon and Rising Sign followed by a deep dive into all of the signs of the zodiac, their planetary rulers and the 12 houses which make up one's birth chart. Then we studied aspects, transits and progressions. We became apprentice astrologers.

Using my own birth chart for reference, I gleaned so much self-understanding in just 6 months of study than perhaps a lifetime of psychotherapy could accomplish. For example, I am an Aquarius Rising. That means at the moment of my birth, the sign of Aquarius was on the horizon...it was rising. Esoteric astrology portends that those of us who have Aquarius on the Ascendant are here to do group work, share, distribute what is needed for the good of the group, be a humanitarian. I love this esoteric phrase for Aquarius - "water of life am I poured forth for all who thirst." Perhaps these poems are my own water of life and I'm pouring them forth for all who thirst for poetry.

As you hold this book in your hands, please know there are no prerequisites for reading it. You don't have to know anything about astrology. You don't need to know anything about poetry. You may choose to read all of the poems cover to cover in one sitting. Perhaps you will choose one poem and meditate on its message today, choosing another for contemplation tomorrow. Personally, I love to use books as an oracle. I ask a question to the Universe, close my eyes then open the book at random to any page knowing that whatever I read at the moment I open my eyes is a message meant just for me, maybe the answer to a question I've been pondering. Try using this book as an oracle just for fun. You may be surprised at what you get for an answer.

I know I speak for most writers when I say I want you to feel something when you read these poems. Inspired. Challenged. Assured. Comforted. Let me know. Did something I wrote speak to a vulnerable part of you? Did a word or a phrase make you want to dive deeper into your own psyche? Did it make you want to learn astrology? Write your own poems? Let me know.

In the meantime, remember this...

> Even the darkest clouds find slumber
> Under the sea of stars
> Only to reveal their silver linings
> That illuminate our every tomorrow.
> And that is the Truth.

Diane DiCola
September 2021

CONTENTS

Poems and Pictures	11
Stellium	13
Untitled 1	14
Untitled 2	16
Untitled 3	18
Untitled 4	20
Moon Music	22
Pardon Me, But I Think Your Yearning is Burning	25
Untitled 5	26
The Moon is Waxing Crescent	28
This is How It All Goes Down	31
Full Pink Moon	32
Our Mother Moon	34
Untitled 6	37
Untitled 7	38
Two Haikus	40

Untitled 8	42
A Honey Moon Love Story	44
We Worship Sun Days	46
Symbol of Life	48
For the Record…	50
It's About Time	52
Untitled 9	55
Untitled 10	56
Acknowledgments	59
About the Author	61

POEMS AND PICTURES

STELLIUM

Together,
We emerge from the darkness and
Approach First Light,
Buoyed by the indomitable strength
Of our healing words
On this voyage of self-discovery.

NOTE: *October 9, 2020 – A stellium is a cluster of 3 or more planets or luminaries (Sun and Moon) that live close together in one single sign or house in one's astrological birth chart. This poem reflects my stellium of Mercury-Mars-Neptune in Scorpio in the 9th House in my chart.*

If you want to see the night
Then follow the Sun
But if you want to feel the light
You must watch the Moon.
When life springs from death
Strong, red and true,
The time is right
To begin.

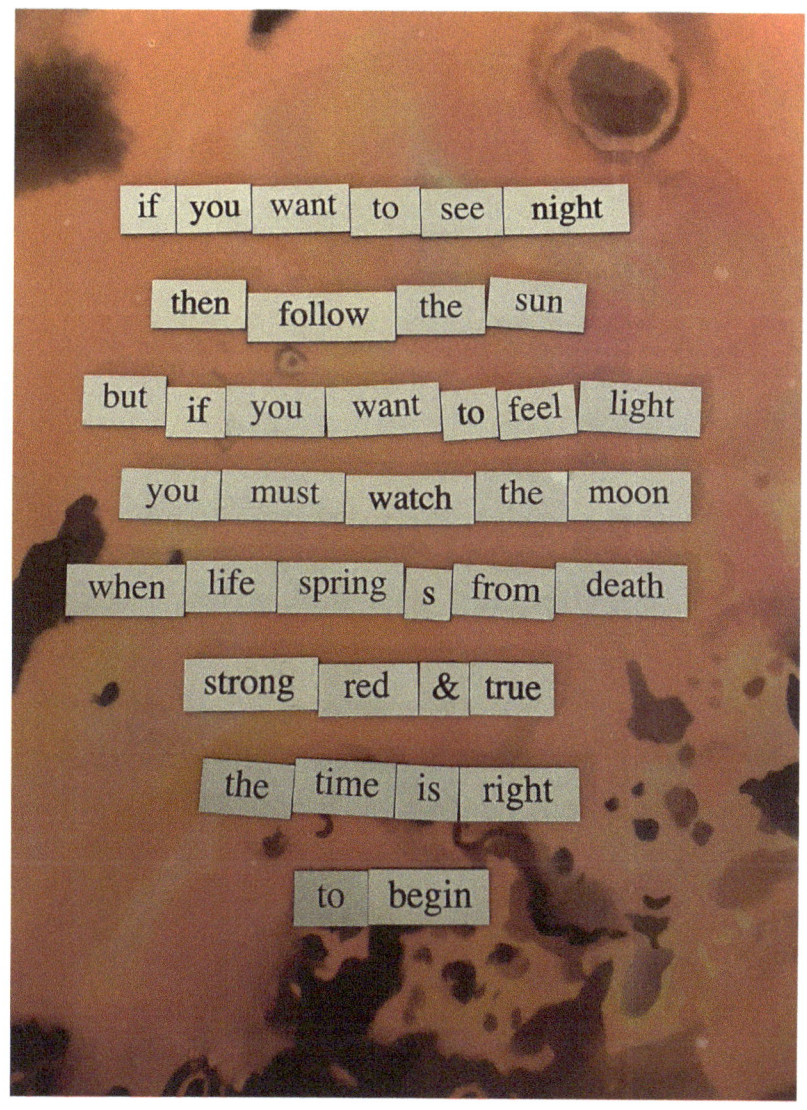

NOTE: *This poem is illustrated on my Mars dinner plate. At this writing, April 11, 2021, the New Moon was in the sign of Aries as were 4 other planets. Mars rules Aries.*

I write wishfully

And hope the winter sky

Will sing my moon song.

NOTE: *January 24, 2021 – This was the first poem I wrote using the Magnetic Poetry® tiles. The background is my refrigerator.*

I imagine

That behind the dark of a long winter night

True love shines bright

Like a secret moon

For you and me.

NOTE: *February 10, 2021 – New Moon in Aquarius. New moons are dark so I used a black cast iron skillet for my background.*

When I ask the goddess mother

To reveal the face of love

She will always whisper

A picture of you

In my dream.

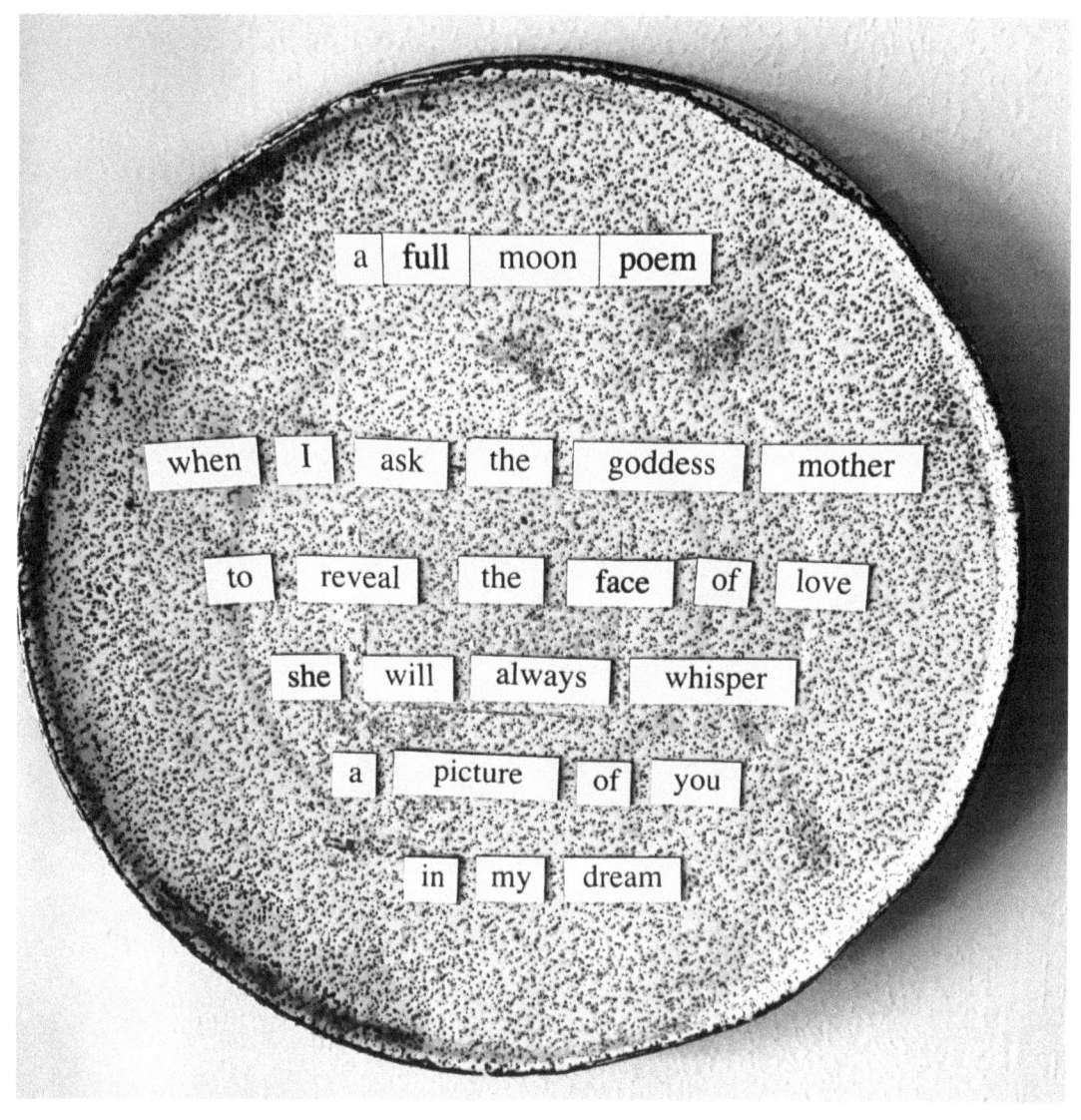

NOTE: *February 27, 2021 – Full Moon in Virgo. The background is the lid from an old Charles Chips® potato chip tin lid.*

MOON MUSIC

Deep within my darkest night
Languid in black diamond light
I long for every song of sea
To see an ocean symphony
Of water spray upon my feet
When winter sings to spring
So sweet.

NOTE: *March 12, 2021 — New Moon in Pisces. This poem was "written" on the bottom side of a black and white speckled bucket to illustrate a starry black sky.*

PARDON ME, BUT I THINK YOUR YEARNING IS BURNING

Each strike of the match
Begins another tale of
Unrequited love.

Smoke signals Heaven
Pleading just this once...
Make me worthy!

NOTE: *March 20, 2021 – I noticed Chiron, the Wounded Healer, in the sign of Aries transiting my 2nd House. Aries is a fire sign and the 2nd House represents what we value, what we want to grow or manifest and our self-worth.*

This moon

Will rise a fever

Of raw hearts pounding

A thousand roses lusting

And us

Heady with want

We spring from our sleep

And play together

In the garden of the Sun

Chanting Love Love Love

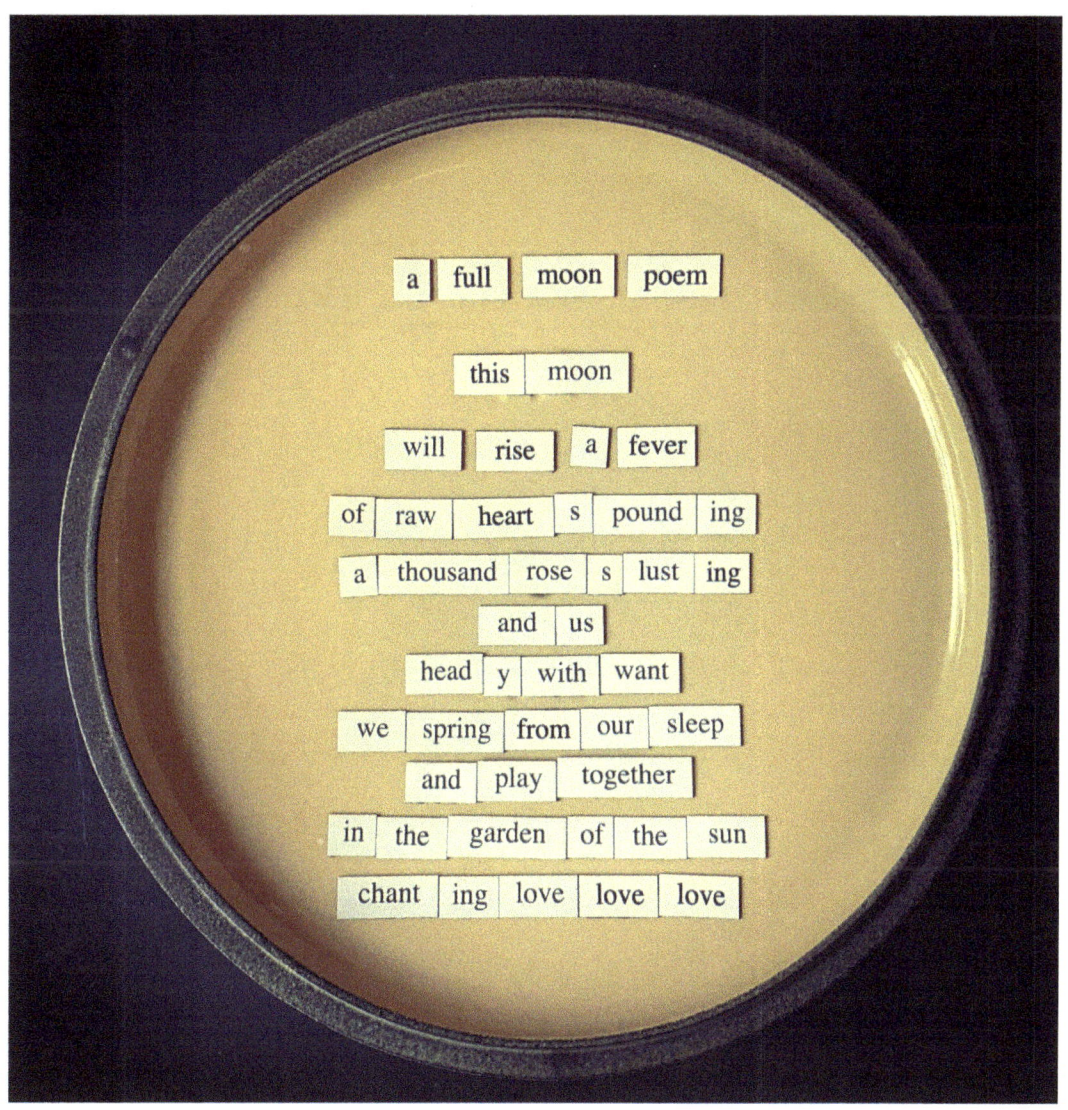

NOTE: *March 28, 2021 — In Aries season, the Full Moon is in Libra. This is the first full moon of Spring. The poem is portrayed on the underside of the lid to my Le Creuset® Dutch oven.*

THE MOON IS WAXING CRESCENT

As wine pours slow

From a spoon

In the sky

I watch petals dance

In the garden.

New life grows

Through earth, old and dry.

I drink it all up and imagine.

NOTE: *April 17, 2021 — This is the only poem I've written for a moon phase other than New or Full. Illustrated on a magnetic chalkboard, the Moon was in Cancer, but it felt more like the Sun was anticipating its move into Taurus in a couple of days.*

THIS IS HOW IT ALL GOES DOWN

First, the sour mash must boil
In a steely cauldron
Before it torrents through spigots
Into thirsty, greedy mugs.
We chase the liquid fire
To the Underbelly
Where it seeks and destroys,
Purging, purifying all matter,
All that mattered.
Essentially
Distilling
Every
Last
Drop.
Then, when Spirit wrangles free,
We raise a glass
And say thank you.

NOTE: *November 11, 2020 – My ode to Pluto, planet of death and rebirth.*

FULL PINK MOON

The journey begins beneath our skin
Deep down below the truth we show
Between the earth and sky by day
Behind a secret self we play.
When inner shadows crush the light
The Moon remembers all that's right
We pray her beauty to reveal
What night transforms
True love can heal.

NOTE: *April 26, 2021 – Full Moon in Scorpio. This poem features sub-tones of Pluto because in some astrology schools, Pluto is another ruler of Scorpio. Also, Pluto stationed retrograde the day after this full moon.*

OUR MOTHER MOON

By touching a delicate petal
She grows a forest of hope
Though strong winds blow
Through trees so new
Her faith sustains their will.
Let her care still frantic breath
And nourish every thing
For it is time to bless the earth
In gratitude we sing.

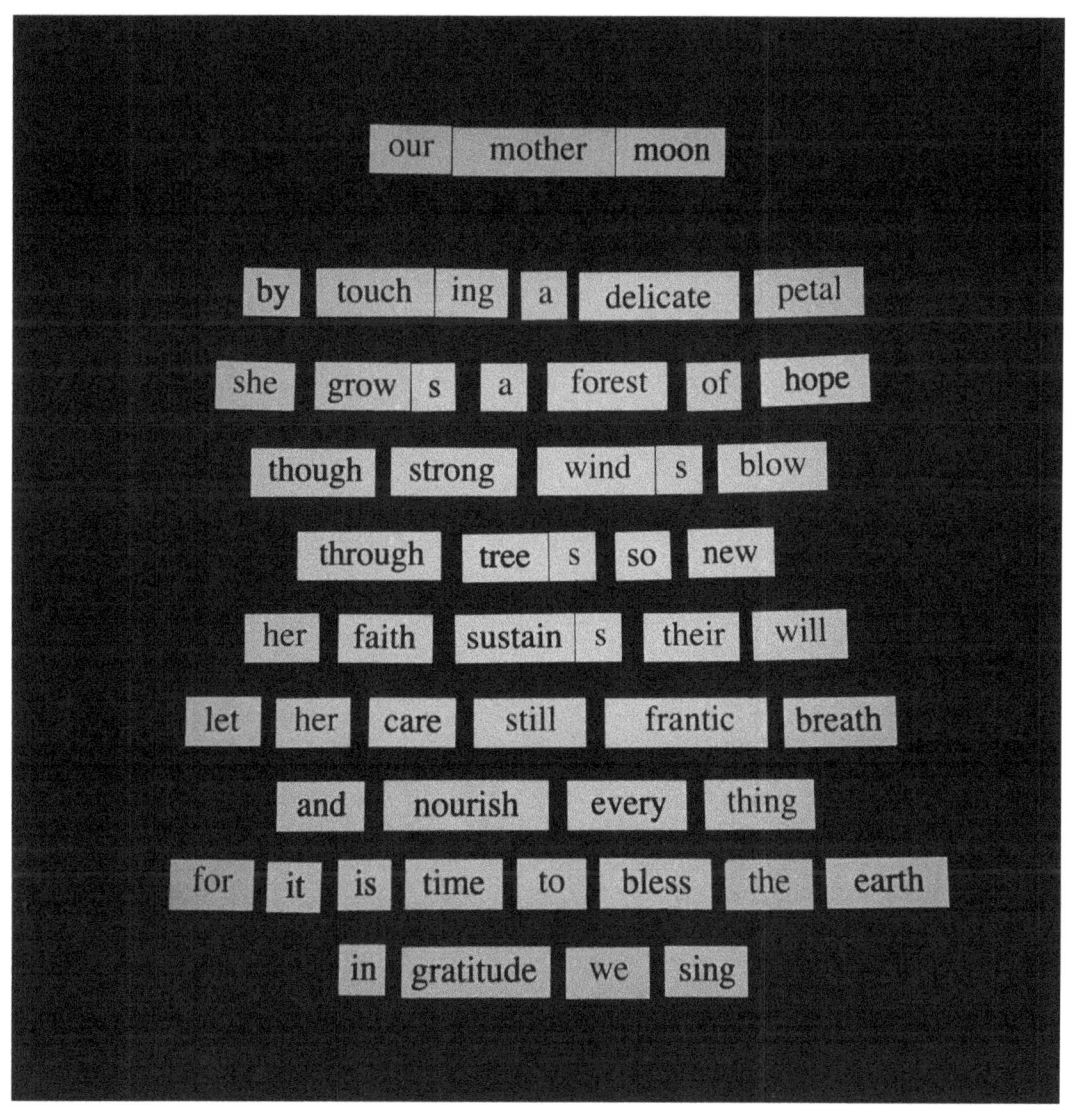

NOTE: *May 11, 2021 – New Moon in Taurus. This poem is illustrated on the inside of a cast iron skillet. "Iron"-Ically, this was my 18th astrology poem I had written and in the traditional Tarot deck, the 18th Major Arcana card is The Moon.*

Sometimes I feel like an undiscovered planet.

When the scientists finally descend upon my mystery,

Will they be thrilled and amazed

Will they hunker down and work to uncover my meaning

Will they conduct tests to determine my origin

Will they account for my rarity

Or will they just acknowledge my existence

and let me be.

Let me be

Ugly, bitter, mean

Then empty the mind

That always makes you remember

How I lie about myself

When the world doesn't understand me.

Trust a song to sing us the answer

And reveal a truth so surreal.

After all,

What appears broken is only playing dead

And we will live to see better days.

We always do.

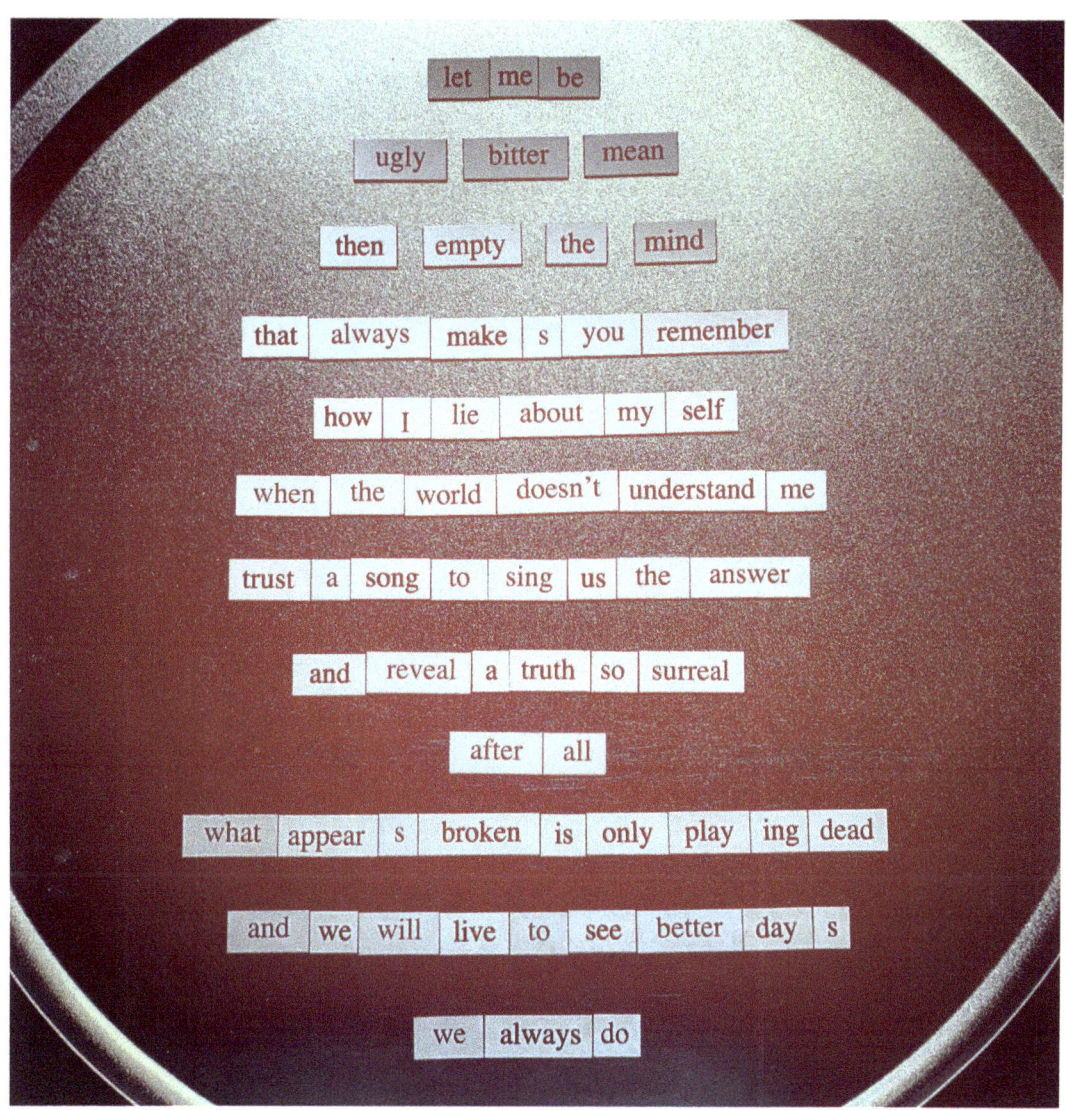

NOTE: *May 26, 2021 – Full Moon in Sagittarius plus a total lunar eclipse. This full moon was also known as the Blood Moon (thus my use of the red filter) and it was a Super Moon. Full moons are times for letting go and this poem conveys release assuring us that better days are coming.*

TWO HAIKUS

I searched for the Moon
But the mystery of you
Escaped with its light.

Dark doesn't live long
Morning opens sleepy eyes
Summer's almost here.

NOTE: *June 4, 2021 — I wrote two haikus because we are in Gemini season. Gemini is the sign of "The Twins." The first haiku is for the New Moon in Gemini which occurred on June 10th and the 2nd haiku anticipates Summer noting the dark of the new moon doesn't last long.*

Look up, sweet love

And imagine a slow summer night

Here at home in my heart

By the light of this perfect full moon.

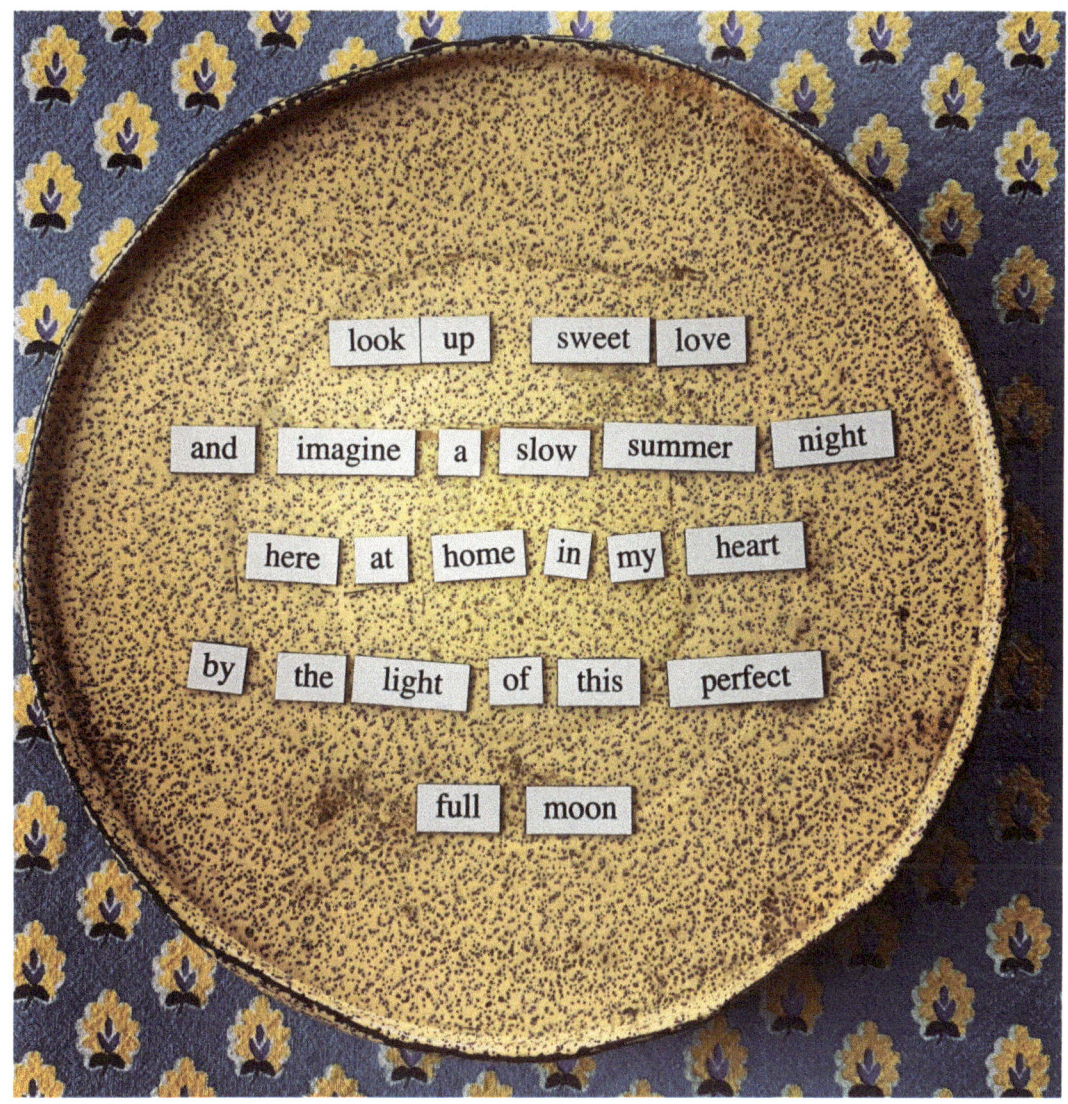

NOTE: *January 28, 2021 – Full Moon in Leo happening in Aquarius season. During winter, we often long for warm summer nights. My full moon is the lid of an old Charles Chips® potato chip tin.*

A HONEY MOON LOVE STORY

One summer night's dream
A man and a woman
Questioned if their love be true.
The Moon said
Live life together in a home
Full of light
Dance, sing and play
Under a sun blooming day
And on a star painted night,
They discovered the answer
Was you.

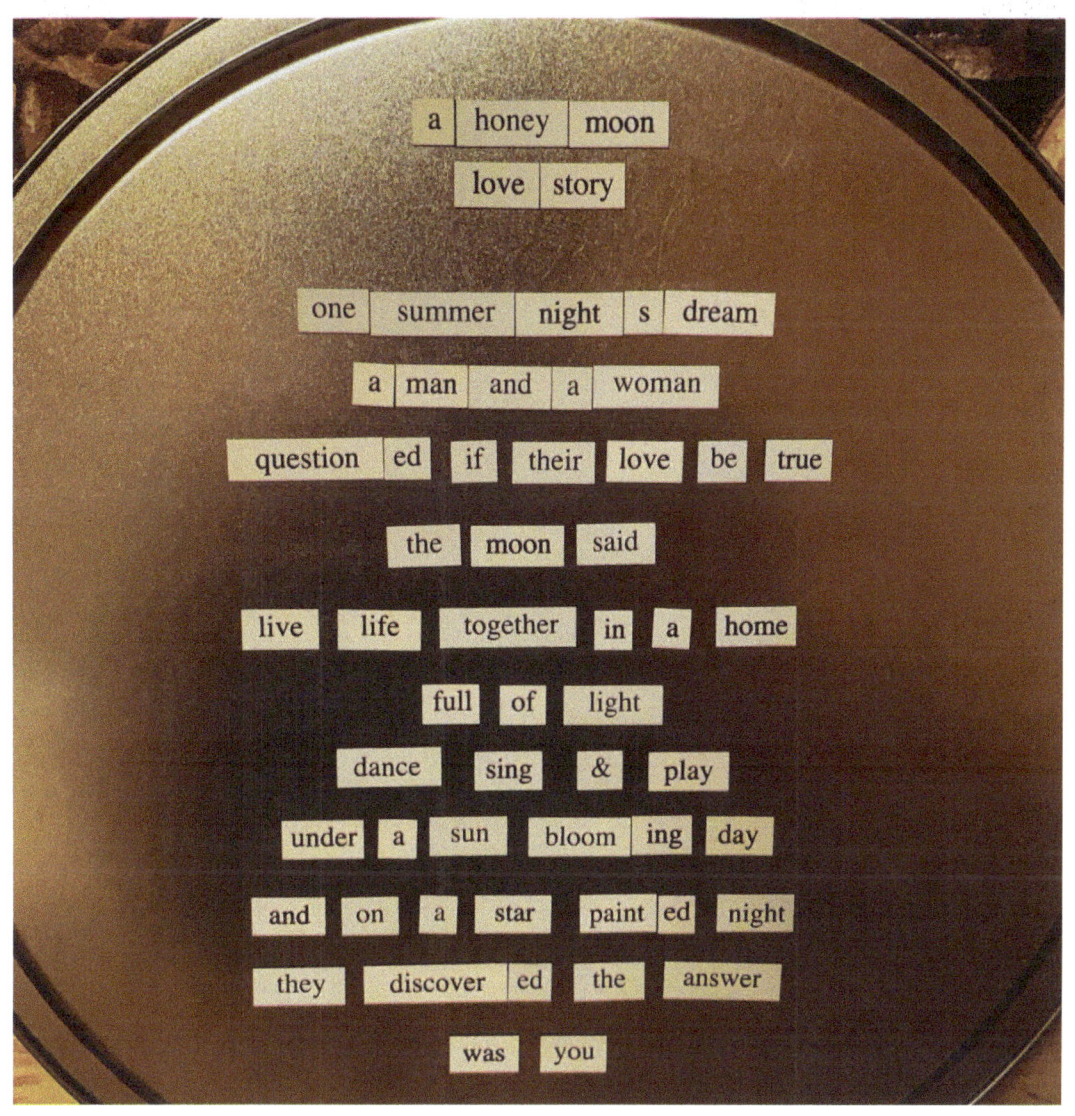

NOTE: *June 24, 2021 – Full Moon in Capricorn during Cancer season. In the zodiac, Cancer is the mother and Capricorn is the father. This poem describes what many parents believe is the greatest expression of their love, a child.*

WE WORSHIP SUN DAYS

She is the favorite song
We sing all summer long
A passion play to the rhythm of our soul
Drink up these days of light
Dance to the beat of your heart
Shine her gift on the world
And let love rule.

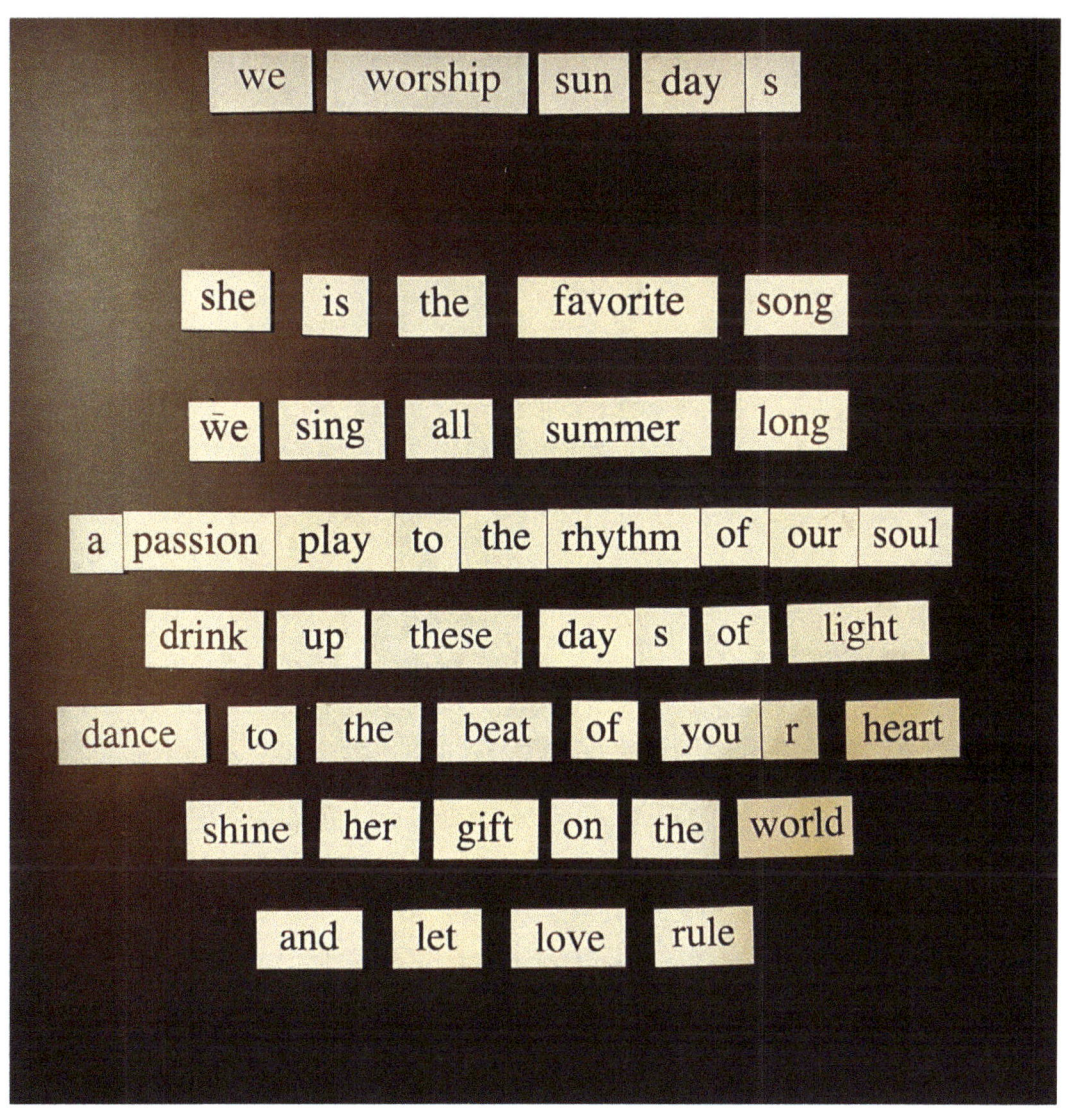

NOTE: *August 1, 2021 — This poem is about Leo season. Leo, the only sign ruled by the Sun, is all about creativity, self-expression and play*

SYMBOL OF LIFE

Water am I
Poured here for all to drink
Wisdom am I
Relief from thoughts we think
Of breath and blood
Of mountain, wind and sun
Friend am I
Together we are one.

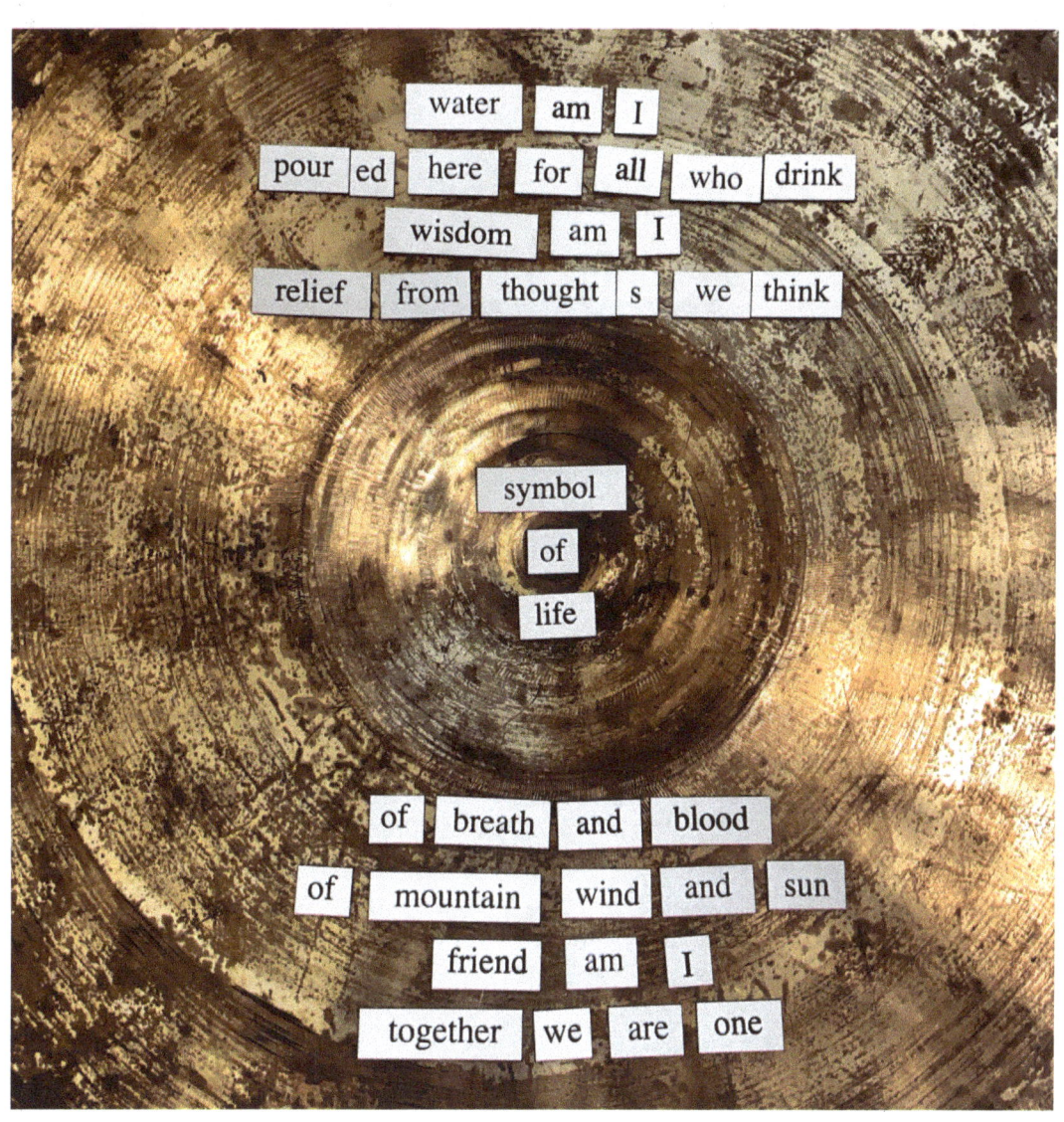

NOTE: *August 21, 2021 — Full Moon in Aquarius occurred on August 22nd, the 2nd full moon in Aquarius during Leo season. This poem is portrayed on my husband's drum cymbal, his idea when I asked for a symbol of a full moon.*

FOR THE RECORD...

When life feels old and broken
She will mend the myth
What was only good without
She makes it better with
Her remedy so pure and true
Hard medicine for some
First believe then you will see
The perfect time has come

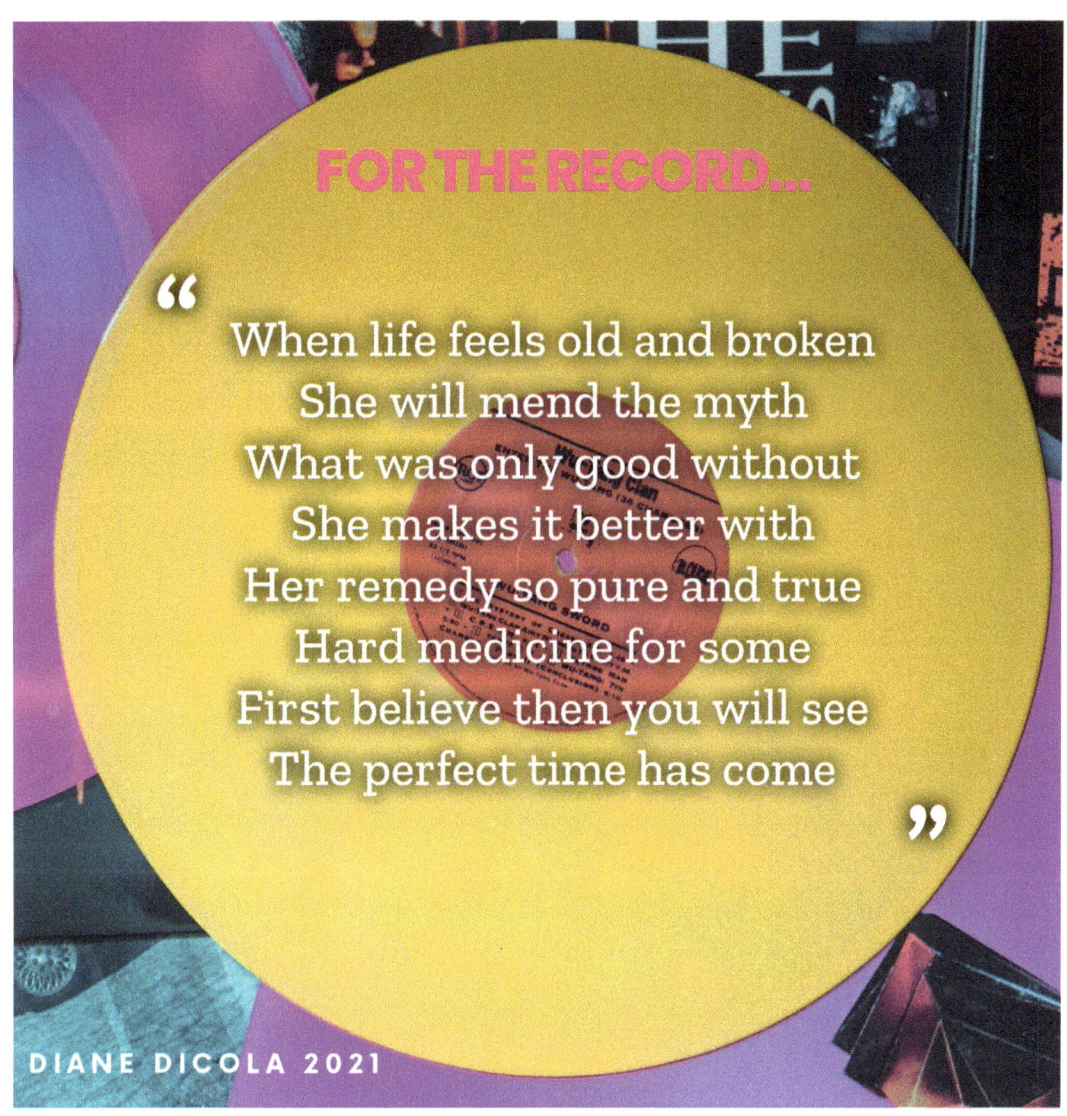

NOTE: *September 6, 2021 – New Moon in Virgo. The background of this photo is an LP, a long playing record. Virgo keeps excellent records. A model of efficiency, she edits, refines and makes things better.*

IT'S ABOUT TIME

Look.

Let me be perfectly clear.

I won't mince words.

This is serious.

It's time.

Now.

Not tomorrow.

Not next week.

Not when you think you're ready.

Now.

You are ready now.

You made a commitment.
You have a responsibility.
You are here to do the work.
Stop wasting time.
This is your time.

Yes, this is hard.
Yes, there are rules.
Yes, you will be tested.
But you are also the foundation
Upon which you build your dreams.
Remember your resolve.

So straighten up.

Buckle down.

Rein it in.

Carpe diem.

It's go time.

Make no mistake.

The time is right.

The time is now.

Right now.

Write now.

NOTE: *The poem is about Saturn conjunct my Ascendant or Rising Sign in Aquarius. Saturn is the planet that governs time, commitment and responsibility. He's the task master, the timekeeper. Once my nemesis, I've come to befriend him and work with his clear and direct energy.*

Remember the wish you prayed
In the deepest of darkest of time,
The hope of a dream come true,
A message from Heaven to shine.
Though its face cannot yet reveal,
You feel it breathing new life
Beneath the dawn of each day
And through the still of the night.
So open your arms to love
Know that love always transcends
The Moon whispers to you in a dream
A new cycle is about to begin.

NOTE: *New Moon in Cancer. Even in times of darkness, there is always hope. There may be no night light during a new moon, but the nurturing love of Cancer welcomes us home and assures us the light is there even if we cannot see it.*

Last night
When the Moon was on fire
A blacksmith forged the dream
Of a fresh start.
You are ready now.

NOTE: *April 12, 2021 – The New Moon in Aries encourages new beginnings and fresh starts. You are ready now.*

ACKNOWLEDGEMENTS

Every morning when I wake up, before my feet hit the floor, I keep my eyes closed and say the following prayer of thanks.

Good morning God, good morning Angels, thank you for this day. Thank you for the sun, the moon, the stars, the planets and my life here on Earth.

Including "the sun, moon, stars and planets" has been there for so many years long before I thought I'd ever write a book in tribute to them. Next, my gratitude often goes towards more specific and more personal considerations such as those of family, health and blessings.

Today, my prayer of thanks includes the following friends.

Heidi Rose Robbins: Author, Teacher, Astrologer, Poet, Friend – Thank you for sharing your knowledge of esoteric astrology and for reacquainting me with the world of poetry and then showing us all how together, their cosmic dance can bring a beautiful new perspective to our everyday world if we're only willing to see it.

Natalie Sack: Writer, Editor, Friend – First, thank you for suggesting that these astrology-inspired poems could be "a thing"…my thing. As facilitator of our monthly writers group, your attention to detail and helpful suggestions to me all these years made you a natural choice to edit this book. Your Scorpion tenacity and Virgoan midwifery brought this tiny book to life with such care and precision.

Writers group members Cynthia Contie, Cora Lee Cole, Judy Laurinatis and Jeff Wesolosky – It is such a pleasure to gather when we do to share our writing samples with each other. I wholly appreciate your comments and suggestions and I'm blessed to be a member of this talented group of writers.

Team at You Can Get It Done Productions – I may have communicated directly with only a few of the amazing individuals on this team, but my heartfelt thanks go to each one of you. Without your encouragement and expert coaching, I may never have brought this book to fruition nor even considered self-publishing.

My family…Kristin, Matt, Rachel, Phil, Ben, Katie, Molly and Alice. Thank you for making me a step-mom and a "D." I love you all!

My Mom and Dad in Heaven – There are no words to express my eternal love and gratitude to you. And no words to tell you how much you are missed. Most days I feel like an old orphan until I get a sign from one of you to let me know that you're still here with me, hopefully proud of what I've accomplished since you've been gone.

Bob – You know how much I love you…but it's even more than that!

You, the reader – Thank you for choosing to read my first book. If you liked it, please share it with someone else who might like a quirky picture book with astrology poems in it. Let's keep lifting each other. This is how we rise up.

ABOUT THE AUTHOR

Diane DiCola is a writer who delights in astrology, numerology, wine tasting and travel. Using her astrological birth chart as a guide to deeper self-understanding, Diane continues to uncover the meaning and purpose of her life with gratitude, wonder and joy.

Drawing upon the virtues of her Libra Sun/Sagittarius Moon/Aquarius Rising blend, Diane shares healing words of hope and grace inspiring us all to create a more peaceful and loving planet Earth.

Written in the Stars is her first book though probably not the last if her storytelling Sagittarius Moon has anything to say about it.

Diane lives with her husband in western Pennsylvania propelled by a not-so-secret dream of a more permanent escape to California or Italy. Meanwhile, you can always find her at DianeDiCola.com.

www.ingramcontent.com/pod-product-compliance
Lightning Source LLC
Chambersburg PA
CBHW061402010526
44119CB00010B/230